# A Picture Book of Louis Braille

David A. Adler

illustrated by John & Alexandra Wallner

Holiday House/New York

To Regina and Allison, with thanks for all your help and encouragement
D.A.A.

To the staff of the Print and Picture Collection of the
Free Library of Philadelphia, with our thanks
J.W. & A.W.

Text copyright © 1997 by David A. Adler
Illustrations copyright © 1997 by John and Alexandra Wallner
All Rights Reserved
HOLIDAY HOUSE is registered in the U.S. Patent and Trademark Office.
Printed and bound in February 2019 at Tien Wah Press, Johor Bahru, Johor, Malaysia.
www.holidayhouse.com
1 3 5 7 9 10 8 6 4 2

Library of Congress Cataloging-in-Publication Data
Adler, David A.
A picture book of Louis Braille/David A. Adler: illustrated by John & Alexandra Wallner.
p.   cm.
Summary: Presents the life of the nineteenth-century Frenchman, accidentally blinded as a child, who originated
the raised dot system of reading and writing used throughout the world by the blind.
ISBN 0-8234-1291-1
1. Braille, Louis, 1809–1852—Juvenile literature.   2. Braille, Louis, 1809–1852—Pictorial works—Juvenile literature.
3. Blind teachers—France—Biography—Juvenile literature.   [1. Braille, Louis, 1809–1852.   2. Teachers.
3. Blind.   4. Physically handicapped.]   I. Wallner, John C., ill.   II. Wallner, Alexandra, ill.   III. Title.
HV1624.B65A64   1997   96-38453   CIP   AC
686.2'82'092—dc20
[B]

Repackaged Edition
ISBN 978-0-8234-4457-1 (paperback)

Louis Braille was born on January 4, 1809, in Coupvray, a
small hillside village near Paris, France. Louis's father was
Simon-René Braille, a saddle maker. His mother was Mo-
nique Baron-Braille. Louis was the youngest of their four
children.

The Brailles lived in a three-room stone house. The food they ate came mostly from their small farm and vineyard. Across the yard, Simon-René had his shop with a large workbench, many pieces of leather, mallets, sharp knives, and pointed awls. While his father worked, Louis often played nearby with small, leftover scraps of leather.

One summer day, while his father was outside with a customer, three-year-old Louis went into the shop. He took one of the sharp-pointed tools he had seen his father use. Louis played with it, imitating what he had seen his father do so often. But the tool slipped and cut into his eye.

Louis screamed. His parents ran to him. They cleaned away the blood and bandaged the eye.

The Brailles took Louis to an old woman who was considered a healer. She put lily water on the wound. Then the Brailles took Louis to a doctor. But there was nothing anyone could do to save the eye. It became infected. The infection spread to the other eye and within a short while Louis Braille was blind.

Louis had to learn again how to feed himself and how to walk without bumping into things.

Louis's father made him a cane. Louis used it to tap the ground in front of him to make sure the path was clear. And when Louis walked somewhere, he counted his steps. He remembered how many there were for his way back.

In his now completely dark world, Louis became more aware of sounds, smells, and the shapes and feel of things. He learned to distinguish the different sounds people made when they walked. He often knew who was coming to the house by the sound their cart made when the wheels rolled over the cobblestone path.

In the early 1800s France was at war. The French emperor Napoleon had sent huge armies to fight across Europe and in Russia. At first they were victorious, but by 1814 the French armies had been defeated and were hurrying back home.

In April 1814 enemy Russian soldiers invaded Coupvray and demanded to be housed and fed. For the next two years many Russian soldiers passed through the Brailles' house. It must have been frightening for young Louis to live with strangers he could neither see nor understand.

In 1815 a new priest, Jacques Palluy, came to Coupvray. He became Louis's first teacher. He taught Louis the Bible. He taught him to recognize animals by their sounds and flowers by their feel and smell.

Louis's father hammered round-tipped upholstery nails into a board to form letters. Louis felt the heads of the nails and learned the alphabet. His father then taught him how to combine letters and form words.

The next year a new schoolmaster, Antoine Becheret, came to Coupvray. It was unusual then for a blind child to attend school. But Louis was especially smart, and Antoine Becheret was anxious to teach him.

Louis could only learn by listening. He couldn't read books the way other children could. Nonetheless, he had a good memory and was an excellent student.

In February 1819 Louis was sent to Paris to live and study at the National Institute for Blind Children. It was the world's first school for the blind, founded in 1784 by Valentin Haüy.

When Louis came to the school, it was in a bleak, five-story building with metal bars on the windows. Thirty years earlier, during the days of the French Revolution, the building had been a prison. Louis Braille would live at the school for the rest of his life.

There were books at the institute for Louis to read. They had raised letters he could feel. The letters were large. The books were big and heavy. Tracing each letter with his fingertips was a slow process. He had to be sure to distinguish between a *P* and an *R*, an *E* and an *F*. But at last Louis was reading.

There were craft and music classes and regular lessons in history, geography, mathematics, Latin, and grammar. Louis especially loved music. He had a real talent for it and learned to play the piano, organ, violin, and cello. Beginning in 1834 Louis played the organ in a few Paris churches.

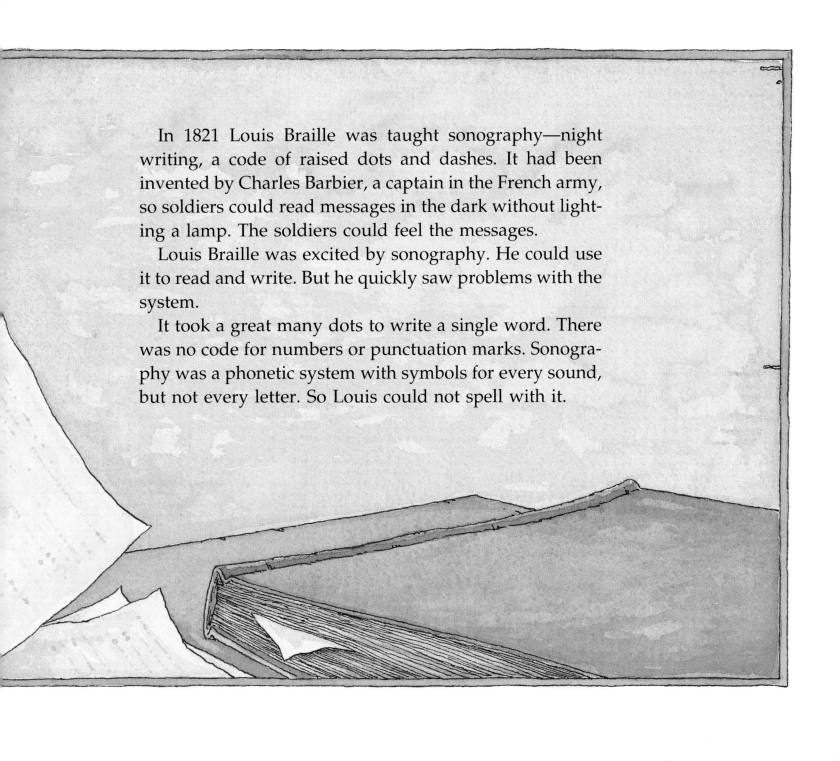

In 1821 Louis Braille was taught sonography—night writing, a code of raised dots and dashes. It had been invented by Charles Barbier, a captain in the French army, so soldiers could read messages in the dark without lighting a lamp. The soldiers could feel the messages.

Louis Braille was excited by sonography. He could use it to read and write. But he quickly saw problems with the system.

It took a great many dots to write a single word. There was no code for numbers or punctuation marks. Sonography was a phonetic system with symbols for every sound, but not every letter. So Louis could not spell with it.

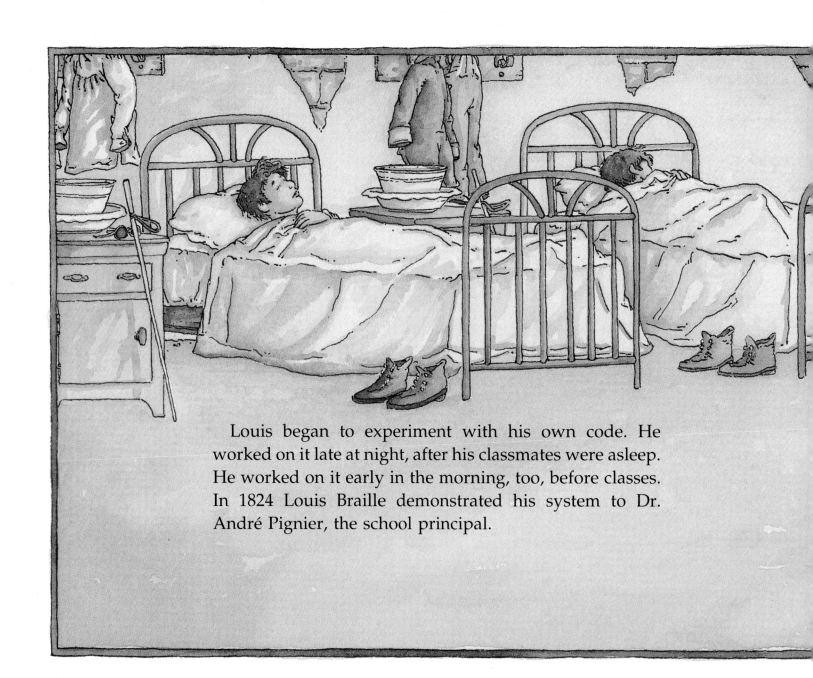

Louis began to experiment with his own code. He worked on it late at night, after his classmates were asleep. He worked on it early in the morning, too, before classes. In 1824 Louis Braille demonstrated his system to Dr. André Pignier, the school principal.

Louis Braille's code used raised dots in two rows of three dots each, like the six dots on a domino. He found sixty-three different combinations—enough for each letter of the alphabet—punctuation marks, numbers, and math signs. Later he developed a raised-dot system for musical notes.

Braille's new system was much easier to learn and read than sonography.

By 1825 Louis Braille and his friend Gabriel Gauthier had made the first braille writing board. Now Louis, Gabriel, and other blind people could write, too.

In 1826 Louis Braille was made an assistant, and two years later a full teacher at the National Institute. He taught mathematics, geography, grammar, and music. While other teachers at the school punished children who did not understand their lessons, Louis Braille was kind and gentle.

At first many sighted people were against switching to Braille's new system. Adopting the new code would be expensive. It would mean new books would have to be produced for the blind. Sighted people had no problems with the old raised-letter system. They could read it easily and saw no need for change.

The National Institute still used the old raised-letter books. But on their own, the students tried Louis's new system. They loved it. Dr. Pignier wanted it adopted at the school. He felt it should become France's official writing code for the blind. But the directors of the National Institute were against it. In 1840, when they found out the school was using books printed in braille, they forced Dr. Pignier to leave the National Institute.

Sighted people were not learning Braille's six-dot system. The blind could not write to them. So in 1839 Louis Braille invented a system he called *raphigraphy*, forming the shapes of letters using raised dots. Blind people could feel the letters. Sighted people could see them.

While Louis Braille worked on his codes, he continued to teach. But in the middle of lessons, he often had to stop. He was having coughing fits. By 1835 his cough developed into tuberculosis, a deadly disease in the 1800s. At times he was too weak to teach. He often went home, to Coupvray, to breathe the clean country air and to rest.

Then, late in 1851, Louis Braille became gravely ill. From his bed he told his friends, "I am convinced my mission on earth is completed." He died on January 6, 1852, just after his forty-third birthday.

The accomplishments of Louis Braille were not widely known in 1852. But by the end of the century, his six-dot code, known simply as "braille," was applied to many languages and was in use around the world.

Helen Keller, who was blind and deaf, called Louis Braille a genius with "godlike courage and a heart of gold." She wrote that braille "made it a pleasure for me to read . . . the world around me shone afresh with treasures." She wrote that Louis Braille "built a large, firm stairway for millions of sense-crippled human beings to climb from hopeless darkness to the Mind Eternal."

# AUTHOR'S NOTE

Today, with proper treatment, Louis Braille's eye injury would not result in blindness. Today there are also medicines to successfully treat tuberculosis, the disease that killed Louis Braille.

Louis Braille first experimented with dots and dashes. When he noticed it was easier to feel just dots, he dropped the dashes.

In 1952, on the one hundredth anniversary of Louis Braille's death, his remains were moved to the Pantheon in Paris. He was laid to rest there among other great French heroes.

# IMPORTANT DATES

1809    Born in Coupvray, France, on January 4.

1812    Blinded in an accident in his father's shop.

1819    Began studies in Paris at the National Institute for Blind Children.

1824    Completed work on his first raised-dot alphabet.

1826    Appointed assistant teacher at the National Institute.

1835    Became ill with tuberculosis.

1839    Invented *raphigraphy*, forming the alphabet with raised dots, so blind people could write to sighted people not familiar with the six-dot system.

1852    Died in Paris on January 6.